Amazing
Bats

WRITTEN BY
FRANK GREENAWAY

PHOTOGRAPHED BY
**JERRY YOUNG
& FRANK GREENAWAY**

Stoddart

A Dorling Kindersley Book

Project editor Christine Webb
Art editor Toni Rann
Senior art editor Jacquie Gulliver
Senior editor Helen Parker
Production Louise Barratt

Illustrations by Ruth Lindsay, Julie Anderson,
and John Hutchinson
Animals supplied by Dr. Uwe Schmidt, Zoologisches Institut, Bonn,
and Trevor Smith's Animal World
Editorial consultant Tony Hutson of the Bat Conservation Trust
Special thanks to Carl Gombrich and Kate Raworth for research

Published in Canada in 1991 by Stoddart Publishing Co. Limited
34 Lesmill Road, Toronto, Canada M3B 2T6

Published in Great Britain in 1991 by Dorling Kindersley Limited
9 Henrietta Street, London WC2E 8PS, England

Canadian Cataloguing in Publication Data
Greenaway, Frank

Amazing bats
(Amazing worlds)
ISBN 0-7737-2501-6
1. Bats - Juvenile literature. I. Young, Jerry.
II. Title. III. Series.

QL737.C5G68 1991   j599.4   C91-093874-1

Color reproduction by Colourscan, Singapore
Printed in Italy by A. Mondadori Editore, Verona

Contents

What is a bat?

Bats are mammals, just like us. They have furry bodies, and wings with no hair. During the day they sleep hanging upside down, and at night they come out to feed.

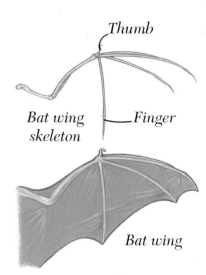

Thumb

Bat wing skeleton —Finger

Bat wing

Ugly mug
This naked bat from Borneo wins the prize for the strangest looking bat of all. Its thick folds of oily skin are a perfect home for earwigs.

Webbed hands
Bats are the only mammals that can fly. Their wings are really webbed hands. Thin, elastic skin stretches right across their very long fingers to their hind legs.

Bat god
The Maya of Central America believed that the underworld was ruled by a bat god. This terrifying god had the body of a human and the head and wings of a bat.

Brown long-eared bat

Little and large
There are almost 1,000 different kinds of bat. The largest are the flying foxes, which are fruit eaters. The smallest bat is only 1 inch long. That's why it is sometimes called the butterfly bat.

Moths or mangoes?
This bat is an insect eater. Like other insect-eating bats, it uses its voice and hearing to find its way in the dark. Fruit bats use their keen eyesight and sense of smell to find their food.

This spear-nosed bat lives in Central and South America

This bat's body is only 3 inches long

Strange flap on nose is called a noseleaf

Fruit eater
This short-tailed spear-nosed bat feeds on fruit. In fact, spear-nosed bats are so good at spotting a tasty meal that they can be real pests on banana plantations.

A bat's thumb is on the edge of its wing. It is small and stumpy, with a useful claw.

Seeing in the dark

Bats don't use their voices just for talking to each other. They also use them to find out what's for dinner – and where it is.

Night shift

When darkness falls, out come millions of nighttime insects. And out come the bats, too. At this time of night, there are plenty of juicy insects for them to eat.

Blind as a bat

Not true! Bats have small but perfectly good eyes. They can see in daylight, just like other mammals.

Signature tune

Each kind of bat has its own call. People who study bats recognize the calls on a bat detector.

Brilliant hearing

Some insect-eaters, like the Bechstein's bat, have huge, sensitive ears for hearing moths and beetles. But fruit bats, which use their *eyes and nose* to find food, have tiny ears.

Fruit bat   *Insect-eating bat*

High squeaks

When a bat goes hunting for insects, it flies along and makes rapid high-pitched squeaks that are too high for most people to hear.

Hello - o - o - o

If these sounds hit an insect, they bounce back like the echo of your voice when you shout in a valley. The bat hears the echo and finds the insect. This clever trick is called echolocation.

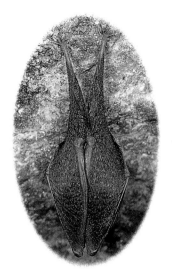

When it is resting, a horseshoe bat folds its wings around its body

Horseshoe bat
The lesser horseshoe bat lives in Europe. It gets its name from the weird flap of skin around its nostrils. Its call is a high, chirping squeak.

You could fit this horseshoe bat into a matchbox

Horseshoe bats can wiggle their ears separately

Squeak again?
Some bats send out strong signals to detect moths or beetles a long way off. Other bats have weaker signals for detecting insects close by.

Bat snacks

Most bats eat insects. But some bats have fruit, nectar, fish, frogs, and other animals on their menus.

Pyramid bat
This mouse-tailed bat is an insect eater. It lives in warm, dry places, even in deserts. In Egypt, the pyramids are a favorite resting-place!

Fruity
Fruit bats live in the hot parts of the world. Their rich fruity colors have led some people to describe them as looking like ripe fruit.

Bat eat bat
The pale ghost bat comes from Australia. Its dinners are often other bats, but it also eats large insects and the occasional bird or two.

Frog muncher
The fringe-lipped bat mainly eats frogs. It can tell the difference between the call of a tasty frog and the call of a poisonous toad.

Going fishing
The bulldog bat from Central and South America trails its extra-long legs in the water and grabs fish with huge hooked claws.

This bat's long, skinny tail is 2 inches long – that's almost as long as its body

Ear ear

The long-eared bat takes particularly large, tasty moths back to its home. It munches the soft body of the moth and lets the wings pile up in a heap below.

Not stupid

Some insects play clever tricks to fool the bats and save their own skin. The china mark moth can tell when a bat is near, and the moth quickly drops to the ground.

Parched lips

Hunting can be thirsty work. This Bechstein's bat swoops down and scoops up water in its mouth.

Where do bats live?

Bats choose all kinds of dark nooks and crannies for their homes. These homes are called roosts. Instead of just one, each bat may have dozens of roosts.

When resting, long-eared bats fold their ears back like accordions

Long-eared bat
Long-eared bats often live in people's attics. They are usually very quiet, and the owners do not know they are there.

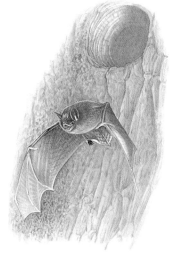

Deep in the forest
Lots of bats live in forests. Hollow trees, woodpecker holes, and fallen logs all provide good hiding places for clusters of bats.

This bat would fit in the palm of your hand

Going camping

The tent-building bat of Central America bites a palm leaf "fan" so that it folds down to make a shelter like a tent.

Living dangerously

In India, one kind of horseshoe bat shares the burrows of the large crested porcupine. Ouch!

Tough bat

The red bat is truly a tree bat. In summer it roosts in tree tops, hanging from a branch in a curled-up ball. And in the freezing winter, some red bats hibernate in trees.

No place like home

A very long time ago, people lived in caves, just like bats. As people learned to make buildings, the bats happily moved in too. Today, bats live in all sorts of places – including houses, castles, and churches.

A lucky charm?

People in Europe used to think that it was unlucky if bats flew into their houses. But bats are welcome visitors to houses in China, where people think they bring good luck.

15

The nursery

When it's time for breeding, mother bats get together and have their babies at the same time. Flying fox nurseries are noisy "camps" in tropical trees. The camps are spread across huge areas and may contain over a million bats.
There is safety in numbers!

Young flying fox

What a lovely baby
A baby flying fox is born with its eyes open, and with a furry coat. The babies of insect-eating bats are born hairless, with their eyes closed. They look like jelly beans.

Mom-eeeee!!
When a mother bat returns to a busy nursery, she finds her baby by its own special call and smell.

Strong hooked claws help this bat cling to branches

This flying fox is 1 foot long, and its wings measure 3 feet from tip to tip!

Mother flying fox

Shh!

Female insect-eating bats have their nurseries in buildings, caves, or hollow trees. These bats are fussy mothers. Conditions in the nursery have to be just right – warm and quiet.

Don't let go

Mother bats can fly with their young when they are tiny. All baby bats have strong feet to help them cling on tightly. But usually, it's much easier to leave baby behind in the nursery.

Apron strings

This female flying fox still has her young baby by her side. It will be able to look after itself by the time it is four months old, but will stay with Mom for much longer.

Practice makes perfect

Baby flying foxes learn to fly when they are four months old. They practise by hanging by their feet and flapping.

Winter breaks

Some bats live in places where there are lots of insects in the summer but none in the long, cold winter. These bats hibernate, or sleep, until warmer weather returns.

Zzzzz . . .
Hibernation is an extra-deep sleep. The bat breathes very slowly, and you might think it was dead. If it is hibernating in a damp cave, a bat may become covered with dew drops.

This noctule's wingspan – the distance from wing-tip to wing-tip – is 15 1/2 inches

Wanted: one cold, damp cave
Bats hibernate in lots of different places. Caves are popular, but some bats use hollow trees or unheated buildings. Word of a good spot can spread, and thousands of bats may end up together!

Noctule bat

This European bat's summer homes are usually no good as winter shelters. It will migrate, or travel, to a suitable winter roost which may be hundreds of miles away.

Hello, sailor

Migrating bats are sometimes caught up in storms and blown far out to sea. They may unexpectedly drop in on ships hundreds of miles from shore.

All tucked in

When they're hibernating, long-eared bats like to tuck themselves in snugly. They fold their long ears back and tuck them under their wings.

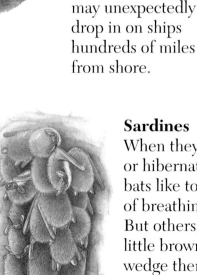

Sardines

When they're resting or hibernating, some bats like to have a bit of breathing space. But others, like these little brown bats, wedge themselves as close together as they possibly can.

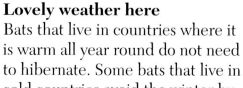

Lovely weather here

Bats that live in countries where it is warm all year round do not need to hibernate. Some bats that live in cold countries avoid the winter by migrating to these warm countries.

Amazing acro-bats

Bats are the acrobats of the air. Using their voices, hearing, and powerful wings, they know just when to swerve, dip, swoop, and soar with silent, graceful movements.

Tail membrane

Netted!
Sometimes bats catch insects in their mouths, but they often use their wings like a net to scoop up prey. Tail membranes make a useful trapping pouch, too.

Twist and turn
Bats are agile fliers and can twist and turn to dart after their prey at great speed – faster than the human eye can follow them.

Sleek bat
When bats hang upside down, they can lick their wings clean and use their thumbs to clean their faces – quite a beauty routine!

This Daubenton's bat has a wingspan of 9 1/2 inches

Tail brake

When they're flying, bats use their tails for balance and for sudden turns and changes of direction. Bats with tail membranes also use them as brakes!

No hanging about

Bats are pretty fast on land, too. They can scoot up a tree trunk or across a cave wall, using their "thumbs" and feet.

Long, narrow wings for flying fast

Fishing bat

The Daubenton's bat likes to hunt over ponds, rivers, and streams which are teeming with insects. It catches flying insects and also plucks them from the water's surface with its big feet.

Gliders

Bats are the only mammals that truly fly, but the colugo comes pretty close! It has a web of skin from wrist to ankle. This helps it glide, rather than fly, from tree to tree.

Vampires

Vampire bats live in the warm tropical countries of Central and South America. By day they sleep in dark caves. At night they come out to feed on the blood of other animals – usually cattle and horses, and sometimes people.

Quietly does it
The vampire bat lands on the ground near its sleeping victim. Silently, the bat hops and creeps up until it is within striking distance.

This tiny vampire bat is only 3½ inches long.

Liquid diet
The vampire bat's top front teeth are razor-sharp. It can quickly bite into a part of its sleeping victim where the skin is thin. As blood flows from the wound, the bat laps it up.

Blood thirsty
The vampire bat sometimes returns night after night to drink from the same animal. It might even move its roost closer to the animal to save the long trip home on a full stomach!

Runny blood

Some vampires drink up to an egg-cupful of blood a night. A substance in the bat's saliva makes the wound go on bleeding long after the bat has finished its meal.

Night prowler

People in Trinidad say that a vampire's bite is really the work of a blood-sucking spirit of the night called a jumbie. By day, they say, jumbies are old women.

False vampires

False vampire bats don't drink blood. They prefer a nice bit of flesh instead. Mice and lizards do just fine!

Open wide

Parts of bats were once used as ingredients in medicines, together with other revolting things like lizards' blood and dogs' tongues!

Enemies

By coming out after dark, bats avoid many would-be enemies. But even in their daytime roosts, they are sometimes at risk.

Spear-nosed bat
This spear-nosed bat from Central America eats mostly fruit and insects. But beware! It has to keep a sharp lookout for a tough relative, a larger spear-nosed bat who would happily catch and eat its small cousin.

This spear-nosed bat's body is about 3 inches long

Lying in wait
The Australian carpet python skulks around below nursery roosts in caves, feasting on baby bats that forgot to hold on tight.

Old timers
If they aren't eaten by other animals or poisoned by mistake, bats can live a very long time. The Daubenton's bat may live for more than 20 years.

Safe spots
In caves or buildings, bats are safest roosting high up in deep crevices. Those roosting or hibernating near the ground are more likely to be snapped up by foxes, martens, or rats.

Wise owl

Barn owls sometimes live in the same cave as bats. They enjoy an occasional bat snack, too.

Bat catcher

In towns and villages, cats are the animals most likely to catch bats.

The colony

Living together has many benefits for bats. The pipistrelles in this cluster can show one another all the best roost, hibernation, and feeding sites in their home range.

Warm and cozy

Mother bats need very warm roosts if their babies are to grow healthy inside them. By clustering together, the bats can make a lot of heat in a small space.

Bat brooch

In warm weather, the roost can become too hot. Baby bats will then crawl off somewhere to cool down. In houses, they might end up almost anywhere. One woman put on a dress and found she had a bat brooch!

A mixed bunch

Winter clusters of hibernating bats need not be a colony. They often come from different places miles apart – and may even be two or three different species.

Hangers-on

One disadvantage of living close together is that parasites – such as fleas and mites – find it easy to move from one animal to another.

Many bats of the same kind, all living and breeding together, are called a colony

Each of these pipistrelles is only 1½ inches long

Pipistrelles

These pipistrelles are so tiny that each one weighs about one sixth of an ounce – that's less than the weight of a quarter.

Caring aunties

Female bats which have no babies often join a cluster and help other bats' babies survive.

Funny faces

The strange lumps and bumps on a bat's face aren't there just for decoration. They help bats give special calls when they're feeding, moving around in the dark, or trying to impress a mate.

This bat measures 8 inches from head to toe

Hammer-headed bat

When they want to attract females, male hammer-headed bats gather in groups called leks and make "honking" noises. The females choose which bat they like best.

Punk bat

This free-tailed bat has a clever way of attracting a mate. It raises its crest of hair and sprays out a scent that's hard to resist.

Long-tongued bat

The long, brushlike tongue of this bat is just what's needed to mop up sweet drops of nectar hidden deep inside flowers.

Slit-faced bats

The slit-faced bat looks more like a rabbit than a bat. It lives in dry parts of Africa, where it roosts in houses, hollow trees, or old burrows.

Tube nose

The nostrils of the tube-nosed fruit bat aren't like ordinary nostrils at all. They stick out like strange, fleshy straws. Nobody knows exactly why they're like this.

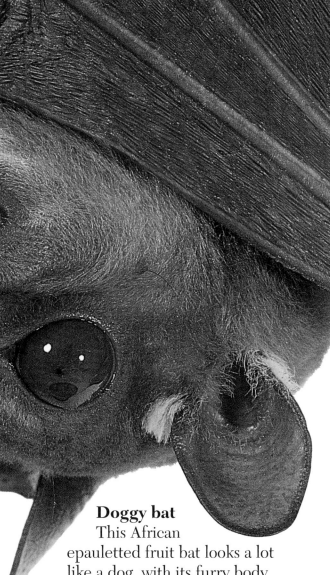

Doggy bat
This African epauletted fruit bat looks a lot like a dog, with its furry body, slender face, and pointed ears.

Wrinkle-faced bat
Because of its wrinkly face, this Central American bat is also called the old man bat. When it hangs upside down, its double chins flap down over its face!

Index